THE STORY OF THE
**TAMPA BAY
DEVIL RAYS**

Published by Creative Education
P.O. Box 227, Mankato, Minnesota 56002
Creative Education is an imprint of The Creative Company

Design and production by Blue Design
Printed in the United States of America

Photographs by Getty Images (Al Bello, Loomis Dean//Time Life Pictures, Otto Greule Jr, Jeff Gross, Tom Hauck, Nick Laham, Scott Jordon Levy/Time Life Pictures, JOHN G. MABANGLO/AFP, Brad Mangin/MLB Photos, Jim McIsaac, PETER MUHLY/AFP, Doug Pensinger, Rich Pilling/MLB Photos, TONY RANZE/AFP, Robert Rogers/MLB Photos, David Seelig/Allsport, Ezra O. Shaw/Allsport, Rick Stewart/Allsport, Ron Vesely/MLB Photos, John Williamson/MLB Photos)

Library of Congress Cataloging-in-Publication Data

Shofner, Shawndra.
The story of the Tampa Bay Devil Rays / by Shawndra Shofner.
p. cm. — (Baseball: the great American game)
Includes index.
ISBN-13: 978-1-58341-501-6
1. Tampa Bay Devil Rays (Baseball team)—History—Juvenile literature. I. Title. II. Series.

GV875.T26S46 2007
796.357'640975965—dc22   2006027456

First Edition
9 8 7 6 5 4 3 2 1

Cover: Pitcher Scott Kazmir
Page 1: Manager Lou Piniella
Page 3: Outfielder Delmon Young

THE STORY OF THE
TAMPA BAY
DEVIL RAYS

by Shawndra Shofner

WADE BOGGS

Tampa Bay Devil Rays

Veteran third baseman Wade Boggs held his bat like a light saber as he stared down Cleveland Indians hurler Chris Haney. Nearly 40,000 fans at Tropicana Field held their breath in anticipation. Haney delivered, and *crack!* the ball arced up, up, and away into the right-field seats. It was August 7, 1999, and Boggs— who had slugged the first home run in the Tampa Bay Devil Rays' inaugural game just a year and a half earlier—had just become the first player in baseball history to smack a round-tripper as his 3,000th hit. To a standing ovation from the roaring crowd, Boggs pumped his fist as he rounded the bases. In an impromptu move that popped the top off the "Trop," Boggs fell to his knees and kissed home plate, placing

an unforgettable exclamation point on a standout career in a city whose name has been synonymous with major-league baseball since 1913.

BASEBALL ON THE BAY

he Tampa Bay area is one of the largest metropolitan areas in Florida and has long-standing historical ties to the game of baseball. Situated on the Gulf Coast, where blue-green water gently sweeps over miles of white sand beaches, Tampa Bay actually refers to a number of towns that surround the body of water known by the same name. The area's two main cities are Tampa and St. Petersburg, but there are a number of smaller cities, including Clearwater, Dunedin, and Bradenton, all of which host major-league teams during spring training.

Tampa Bay's climate makes it ideal for early-season baseball, and 19 major-league teams have called the Bay area their spring training home. The Chicago Cubs became the first when they moved their training headquarters from New Orleans to Tampa in 1913. A year later, the St. Louis Browns moved their spring workouts to St. Petersburg. An exhibition game in 1914 between the Cubs and Browns initiated the Grapefruit League, a five-week series of preseason games between teams that train in Florida. The Grapefruit League came to include 18 teams, including the St. Louis Cardinals, New York Giants, New York Mets, Los Angeles Dodgers, and Cleveland Indians. The only in-

GRAPEFRUIT LEAGUE – Warm sunshine, green grass, and the crack of bat on ball has long lured fans from snowy regions southward in the spring. Florida's Grapefruit League has included many of baseball's most successful teams, from the Yankees to the Pirates.

terruption to this spring tradition was World War II (1942–45); during these years, baseball commissioner Kenesaw Mountain Landis restricted teams from training west of the Mississippi River or south of the Potomac River so that the railways could remain open for troops and supplies.

Because of its reputation as a baseball destination, Florida's west coast soon became a bargaining tool for major-league teams seeking new ballparks or renovations to their existing sites. In the 1980s, the Minnesota Twins, Oakland Athletics, Chicago White Sox, Texas Rangers, Seattle Mariners, and San Francisco Giants all threatened to relocate to the Bay area unless they were given stadium upgrades. Rather than lose their franchises, the cities gave the teams what they wanted.

In 1986, in an effort to make the area more attractive to either an expansion team or an existing franchise looking for a new home, Bay area officials approved construction of the 45,200-seat Florida Suncoast Dome, a cable-supported, domed stadium in St. Petersburg. Unfortunately, the draw of the new dome was not enough when, in 1991, Major League Baseball decided that Denver and another Florida locale, Miami, were better suited to host expansion teams. Later attempts to lure the Mariners and Rangers fell through, but baseball hopes soared in 1993 when local businessman Vincent J. Naimoli agreed to purchase the Giants and relocate them to Tampa Bay. However, a legal loophole allowed a California investment group to purchase the Giants

ALL-TIME TEAM

PITCHER · VICTOR ZAMBRANO

Right-hander Victor Zambrano's pitching repertoire included a blurry 94-mile-per-hour sinking fastball, a challenging changeup, and a slippery slider that was virtually unhittable. In 2003, Zambrano held opponents to a .237 batting average, fifth-lowest in the AL, and became the Devil Rays' all-time leader in wins (35) and strikeouts (372). However, the Venezuelan had a wild side as well, leading the AL in walks, wild pitches, and hit batsmen in 2003. His watchfulness and quick reflexes on the mound made him a difficult pitcher to steal against, and he kept base runners wary with his quick pickoff throws.

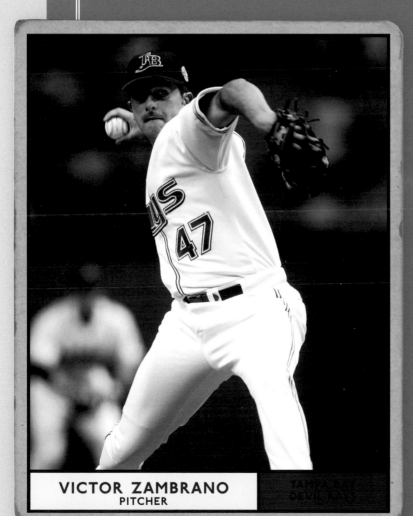

VICTOR ZAMBRANO
PITCHER

TAMPA BAY
DEVIL RAYS

STATS

Devil Rays seasons: 2001–04

Height: 6-0

Weight: 205

- **513 career strikeouts**

- **45–41 career record**

- **4.45 career ERA**

- **.932 career fielding percentage**

TAMPA BAY'S HOME TURF

When a ballclub failed to take up residence at Florida Suncoast Dome, the National Hockey League's Tampa Bay Lightning franchise moved to the empty stadium in 1993 and changed its name to the Thunderdome. Three years later, the Lightning built a new arena, the Ice Palace, and the owners of the Thunderdome converted it back to a ballfield to accommodate the expansion Devil Rays. Renamed Tropicana Field after a deal with the juice-making sponsor added $13 million to the city of St. Petersburg, the revamped park offered all-dirt base paths and FieldTurf, a natural-looking synthetic grass. An eight-story-high mosaic containing 1.8 million color tiles depicting the sun, sea, and beach welcomed guests, who might visit a café located directly behind the Rays' bullpen in the right-field corner; a spa at "The Beach," a concourse on the second level off of left field complete with palm trees and employees wearing Hawaiian shirts; or a climbing wall on the Center Field Street concourse. The world's second-largest cable-supported domed roof, built to withstand hurricane gales of up to 115 miles per hour, was lit a luminous orange when the Devil Rays won a home game.

instead, keeping them in San Francisco.

On October 15, 1997, Major League Baseball approved a resolution creating a 16-team National League (NL) and a 14-team American League (AL) for the 1998 season. Tampa Bay was awarded a franchise and placed in the AL's Eastern Division, at last ending what Naimoli called "a path of ten thousand steps, ten thousand phone calls, ten thousand frustrations." Finally, the area that had hosted other cities' teams for almost 100 years had a team to call its own.

LARRY ROTHSCHILD – While the Devil Rays' formation entered its final stages in October 1997, Larry Rothschild was helping coach the Florida Marlins to a world championship. One month later, Rothschild was named the first Tampa Bay skipper.

CATCHER · TOBY HALL

Toby Hall split time between the Devil Rays' big-league roster and minor-league teams between 2000 and 2002 before he was finally named full-time catcher for Tampa Bay in 2003. On August 20 of that season, he homered in the top of the ninth inning off of Seattle Mariners pitcher Shigetoshi Hasegawa to give Rays manager Lou Piniella a 60th birthday present: a 3–2 win. The burly catcher, who often wore a red beard and was known for his strong arm, threw out 43 percent of would-be base stealers in 2003 and drove in a career-high 60 runs in 2004.

STATS

Devil Rays seasons: 2000–06

Height: 6-3

Weight: 205

- **.265 career BA**

- **44 career HR**

- **259 career RBI**

- **.989 fielding percentage**

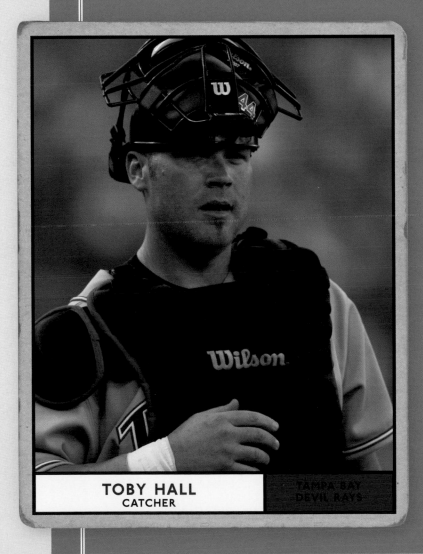

TOBY HALL
CATCHER

TAMPA BAY
DEVIL RAYS

DEVIL RAYS DEBUT

 telephone "name-the-team" contest that generated more than 70,000 calls from Tampa Bay residents resulted in the new franchise being named the "Devil Rays." A common sight in the Bay waters, devil rays (also called manta rays) are odd-looking marine creatures that get their name from unique fins on their heads that resemble devil's horns. The team's uniforms were soon unveiled in tones of black, green, and blue. In July 1995, just months after the new team was officially created, Chuck LaMar was named the Devil Rays' general manager. Known for his ability to find talent and build championship teams, LaMar had previous experience with the Cincinnati Reds, Pittsburgh Pirates, and Atlanta Braves. "I am extremely pleased to join an organization that in the coming years will become one of the class franchises in major league baseball," LaMar said.

Larry Rothschild, a respected major-league pitching coach who had never before managed a game, was named the team's manager. The Devil Rays made their first major-league trade on November 11, 1997, acquiring lanky outfielder Mike Kelly from the Reds. "I was thrilled," said Kelly, "because I knew it meant I was getting an opportunity to play, and that's what it's all about."

Mike Kelly spent just one season in Tampa Bay, achieving career highs with 10 home runs and 13 steals.

MIKE KELLY

Two weeks later, the Devil Rays used their first pick in a special expansion draft to select pitcher Tony Saunders, who had been a member of the World Series-winning Florida Marlins the year before. By the draft's conclusion, the Rays had selected 35 players, including quick, compact center fielder Quinton McCracken, who had stolen 28 bases for the Colorado Rockies in 1997, and catcher Mike Difelice from the St. Louis Cardinals.

After the draft, Tampa Bay continued to add talent via trades and free agent signings. The Rays acquired hard-hitting first baseman Fred "Crime Dog" McGriff, a Tampa native, through a trade with the Braves and signed free agent pitcher Roberto Hernandez. They also swung a trade for shortstop Kevin Stocker and signed free agent pitcher Wilson Alvarez. "It's been the most exciting week I can remember," said LaMar, "to sit down with the 28 other general managers for the first time and talk trades."

The Devil Rays debuted before a sold-out Tropicana Field crowd on March 31, 1998. Playing against the Detroit Tigers, the Devil Rays lost 11–6 but returned the next day to best Detroit with hits in every inning

KEVIN STOCKER

PAUL SORRENTO

A DEVILISH FIRST GAME

The Devil Rays' first regular-season game at home on March 31, 1998, commenced when Wilson Alvarez threw the first pitch to Detroit Tigers leadoff hitter Brian Hunter. Alvarez retired the first three batters but soon ran into trouble, allowing six runs and nine hits before vacating the mound in the middle of the third inning. Relief pitcher Dan Carlson fared little better against the Tigers, and by the fifth inning, Detroit led 11–0. But the Devil Rays refused to submit to defeat that easily. Veteran third baseman Wade Boggs hit a home run off of Detroit pitcher Justin Thompson to score the first two runs in Devil Rays history. The sold-out crowd went wild when Tampa Bay rallied to score four more runs in the ninth. With two outs and the bases loaded, designated hitter Paul Sorrento approached the plate. Fans crossed their fingers. A grand slam would bring the Rays within one run of tying the game. Sorrento swung for the fences but struck out, and the game ended 11–6. "We made it interesting," Tampa Bay right fielder Dave Martinez said. "But that's pretty much the character of this team. We went through spring training showing that we won't give up."

ROBERTO HERNANDEZ

One of the game's top closers, Roberto Hernandez set a team record with 43 saves during the 1999 season.

FIRST BASEMAN · FRED McGRIFF

Tampa Bay acquired offensive powerhouse Fred "Crime Dog" McGriff from the Atlanta Braves in its inaugural season. A feared fastball hitter with a smooth swing, the lanky first baseman delivered 32 homers for the Devil Rays during the 1999 season, and in 2000, he slugged 27 more, including the 400th of his career. In a 2000 game against the Baltimore Orioles, the Tampa native hit a home run in his 37th different ballpark. He signed with the Rays again in 2004, hoping to hit nine homers and reach the prestigious 500 mark, but retired in July after hitting only two.

FRED McGRIFF
FIRST BASEMAN

TAMPA BAY
DEVIL RAYS

STATS

Devil Rays seasons: 1998–2001, 2004

Height: 6-3

Weight: 215

• **5-time All-Star**

• **2-time league leader in HR**

• **1994 All-Star Game MVP**

• **493 career HR**

SECOND BASEMAN · MIGUEL CAIRO

For the first three years of the Devil Rays' existence, Venezuelan Miguel Cairo manned second base for the young franchise. In 1999, the keen-eyed Cairo ranked as the AL's eighth-most difficult strikeout target, getting "K'd" only once every 11 plate appearances on average and posting a .295 batting average with a 12-game hitting streak. Renowned for his accurate throws and wide-ranging fielding ability, he posted the league's third-highest fielding percentage in 2000. Cairo also displayed impressive speed on the base paths, swiping a team-record 28 bases that same season, including two in one inning against the Seattle Mariners.

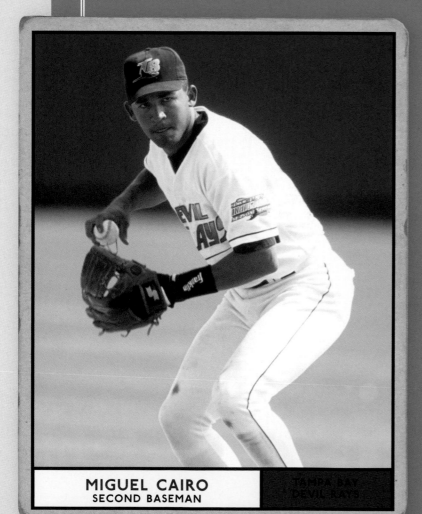

MIGUEL CAIRO
SECOND BASEMAN

TAMPA BAY
DEVIL RAYS

STATS

Devil Rays seasons: 1998–2000

Height: 6-0

Weight: 160

• **.981 career fielding percentage**

• **.328 playoff BA**

• **280 career RBI**

• **113 career stolen bases**

except the fifth. With Cuban pitcher Rolando Arrojo in control on the mound and McGriff driving in four runs on three hits, the Rays thrilled their fans with a retributive 11–8 victory.

On April 13, the Rays entertained the hometown faithful again with a 14-inning nail-biter. Facing the Minnesota Twins, the Devil Rays trailed 7–1 before scoring five runs in both the sixth and seventh innings. The Twins answered back, and after nine innings, the teams were tied 12–12. Finally, after 4 hours and 54 minutes, feisty Devil Rays third baseman Bobby Smith smacked his first major-league home run in the bottom of the 14th inning to give the Rays a 13–12 win.

By mid-April, the Devil Rays were the first expansion team ever to be four games over .500 in their inaugural season with a 10–6 record. But despite the promising start and solid contributions from Arrojo, McCracken, McGriff, and youngsters such as Smith and rangy outfielder Randy Winn, the Devil Rays fell into last place in the AL East and stayed there, finishing the season with a 63–99 record.

Tampa Bay started its second year a very respectable 22–20. Much of that season's excitement came from veteran players achieving career milestones in Devil Rays uniforms. For example, strapping outfielder Jose Canseco, who had signed with the Devil Rays before the start of the season, blasted his 400th career home run on April 14, 1999, in Toronto against his former team,

A GAME WITH TWO ENDS

The Devil Rays were ahead 4–3 with two outs in the bottom of the ninth inning on May 31, 2000, when Baltimore Orioles outfielder B.J. Surhoff hit a grounder to Rays shortstop Felix Martinez. Martinez fired a one-hopper to Fred McGriff at first, first base umpire Brian Runge called Surhoff out, and the Rays started to celebrate. But Orioles manager Mike Hargrove and first base coach Eddie Murray argued Runge's call, pointing to an off-the-bag footprint left by McGriff. Nine minutes later, umpire crew chief John Shulock overruled Runge's call, and both teams were called back onto the Tropicana field to finish the game. An angry Devil Rays manager Larry Rothschild considered forfeiting the game but agreed to play in protest. "I don't understand it," Rothschild said. "Yeah, get the call right. But don't let us get off the field and the whole thing. Do you watch a replay after the game and decide you made a bad call so let's go replay it tomorrow?" When the game resumed, Orioles center fielder Charles Johnson hit a single to right field, advancing Surhoff to third. Outfielder Brady Anderson then drew a full count before striking out on a Roberto Hernandez fastball, and the Rays won the one-of-a-kind game—again—4–3.

THIRD BASEMAN · JORGE CANTU

Jorge Cantu, who signed with Tampa Bay in 1998 when he was just 16 years old, was called up from Durham, the club's top minor-league team, to start for the Devil Rays in 2004. "We thought he could hit 15 home runs [and] drive in 70 runs, but he superseded everything we expected," said Tampa Bay manager Lou Piniella after Cantu put up 28 dingers and 117 RBI in 2005. Cantu exceeded his mother's expectations, too, when he followed through on a home run promise to her on Mother's Day in 2005 by hitting his first walk-off round-tripper in a game against the Chicago White Sox.

JORGE CANTU
THIRD BASEMAN

TAMPA BAY
DEVIL RAYS

STATS

Devil Rays seasons: 2004–present

Height: 6-1

Weight: 185

- **326 career hits**

- **78 career doubles**

- **.275 career BA**

- **196 career RBI**

JOSE CANSECO

JOSE CANSECO – Although his reputation was later tarnished by admissions of steroid use, Canseco was a crowd-pleasing slugger throughout the 1990s. He made up for weak fielding skills by slugging 462 round-trippers over the course of his career.

the Blue Jays. Fans also went wild on August 7 when third baseman Wade Boggs, a Tampa native, became the first player in the history of baseball to pop a home run for his 3,000th career base hit.

Such individual heroics were not enough to keep the team afloat, however, as the Devil Rays suffered more injuries than any other team in the major leagues that season, putting 18 players on the disabled list for the incredible combined total of 873 days. As the losses mounted, fan support dwindled. Average attendance at Tropicana Field dropped below 20,000 a game, even though the team showed modest improvement by going 69–93.

Quinton McCracken had electrifying speed before suffering a torn knee ligament early in the 1999 season.

QUINTON McCRACKEN

TREADING WATER

n an effort to make the 2000 team more competitive, the Devil Rays fished for some affordable big-name players in the off-season. They thought they caught their limit when they netted two heavy hitters: power-packed third baseman Vinny Castilla and three-time All-Star outfielder Greg Vaughn, both of whom came over from NL teams. "I'm not a savior by any means," said Vaughn, who had slammed 45 home runs and collected 118 runs batted in (RBI) for the Cincinnati Reds the year before. "I'm just a small piece of the puzzle. Those [other] guys are pretty good players. I think we have a pretty good shot at doing some things."

With the additions, the club's lineup suddenly consisted of powerhouse hitters McGriff, Canseco, Vaughn, and Castilla. Excited Tampa Bay fans quickly nicknamed the foursome "Murderers' Row" since the quartet had combined for 144 homers in 1999. Hopes quickly evaporated, however, when instead of blasting balls out of the park, three of the four sluggers suffered slumps and injuries. Castilla popped a meager six home runs and batted only .221 before injuries landed him on the disabled list. Vaughn, too, spent weeks on the disabled list, and Canseco was released before the end of the year.

GREG VAUGHN – Vaughn (right) batted a mere .242 for his career. But the outfielder and designated hitter was more interested in home runs than a high average. Unfortunately for Tampa Bay fans, most of his power had been spent by the time he arrived in 2000.

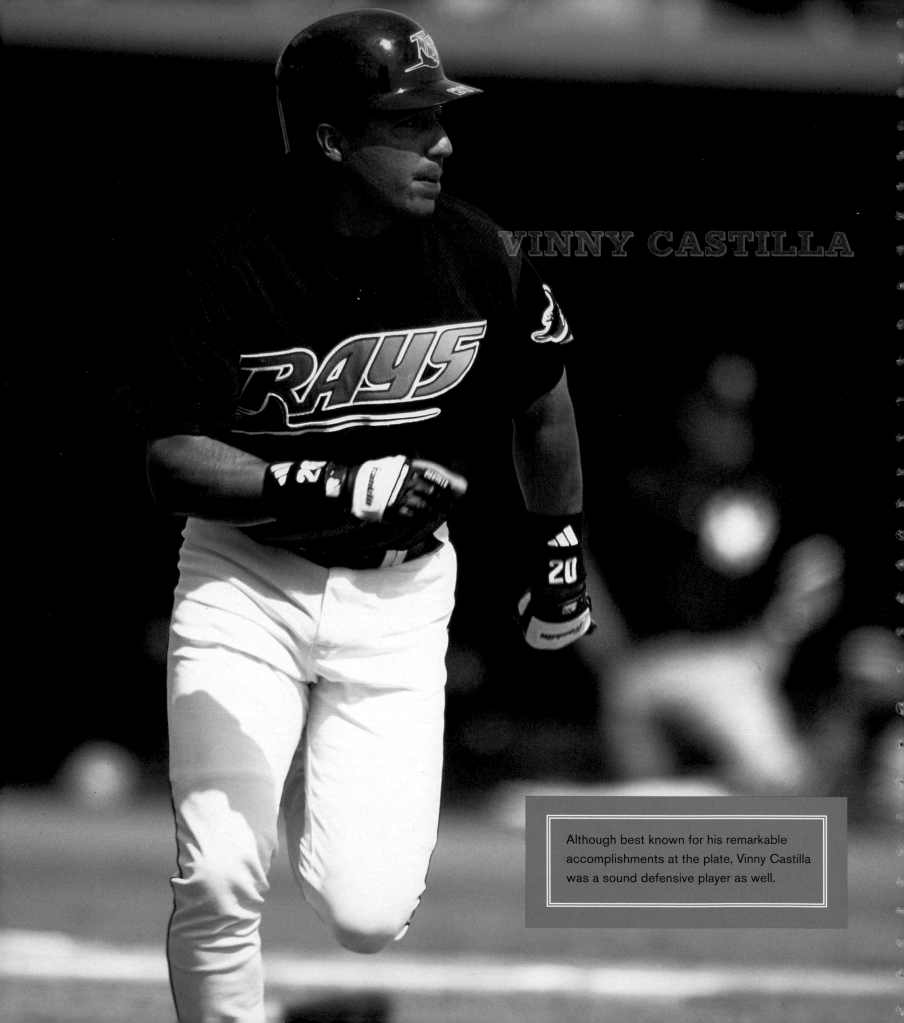

VINNY CASTILLA

Although best known for his remarkable
accomplishments at the plate, Vinny Castilla
was a sound defensive player as well.

SHORTSTOP · JULIO LUGO

Dominican-born Julio Lugo, who moved to New York City when he was 12, took over as the Devil Rays' shortstop in May 2003. In 2004, he showed dramatic improvement as a hitter, driving in a career-best 75 runs and leading the Rays in batting with runners in scoring position. He was a versatile hitter, equally adept at driving the ball into outfield gaps, dropping bunts for infield singles, or slapping the ball through the infield on hit-and-runs. In July 2005, he set a team record for hits in a month with 40. Lugo's speed and aggression also made him a valuable base thief.

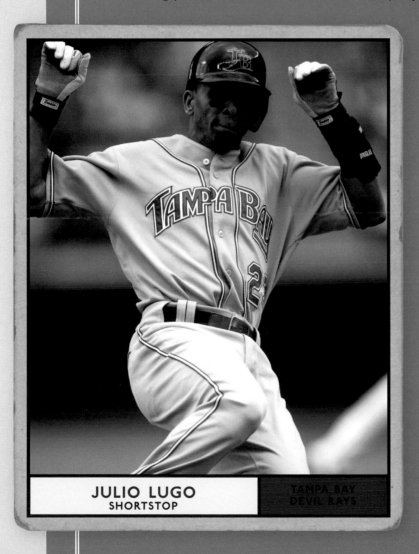

JULIO LUGO
SHORTSTOP

TAMPA BAY
DEVIL RAYS

STATS

Devil Rays seasons: 2003–06

Height: 5-10

Weight: 165

- **.277 career BA**

- **936 career hits**

- **336 career RBI**

- **139 career stolen bases**

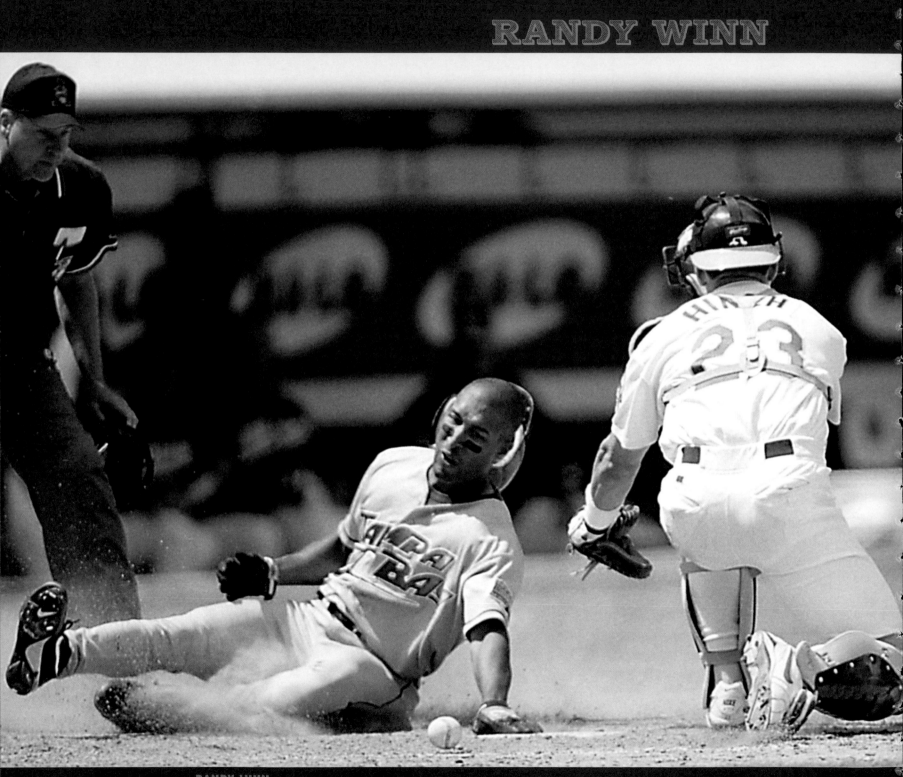

RANDY WINN – The fleet-footed outfielder's best season in Tampa Bay was his final one (2002). That year, he stole 27 bases, scored 87 runs, and earned his first appearance in an All-Star Game. He was the team's only representative in the "Midsummer Classic."

Only McGriff finished the 2000 season healthy, putting up 106 RBI. In September, the team limped through a 2–16 stretch despite some solid pitching by hurlers Albie Lopez, Bryan Rekar, and Esteban Yan. The Devil Rays ended the season in last place in the AL East once again with a 69–92 mark.

Hoping to shake loose of their struggling ways, team management made sweeping changes in 2001. The club traded away Hernandez and pitcher Cory Lidle and brought Ben Grieve—an up-and-coming outfielder formerly with the Oakland Athletics—to town. Next, Tampa Bay fired Larry Rothschild in April after a 10–0 loss to the Boston Red Sox and replaced him with Rays bench coach Hal McRae. Known for his intense personality, McRae rose to the challenge, stating a litany of simple goals for his club. "We're going to catch it, hit it, and throw it better," said McRae. "Our players will be on time, play hard, play to win, and play unselfish baseball."

The changes continued as Tampa Bay dismantled its lineup of struggling heavy hitters, releasing Castilla and trading McGriff to the Chicago Cubs for 24-year-old infielder Jason Smith. Vaughn, the only one of the big boppers that remained, batted a miserable .233 with just 24 homers in 2001. Even though the Rays played better ball in the latter part of the season, the team racked up a whopping 100 losses, finishing in last place again and

LEFT FIELDER · CARL CRAWFORD

Even though he never played organized baseball before entering high school, Carl Crawford was named a Second-Team All-American by *Baseball America* magazine in his senior year in 1999, and turned down college athletic scholarships for basketball and football to play baseball. He was drafted by Tampa Bay, and after three years in the minor leagues, the speedy 21-year-old was called up to the "big show" in the middle of the 2002 season. By season's end, he had earned Tampa Bay's Most Outstanding Rookie honors, and in 2003 and 2004, he stole 114 combined bases, leading the AL in steals each season.

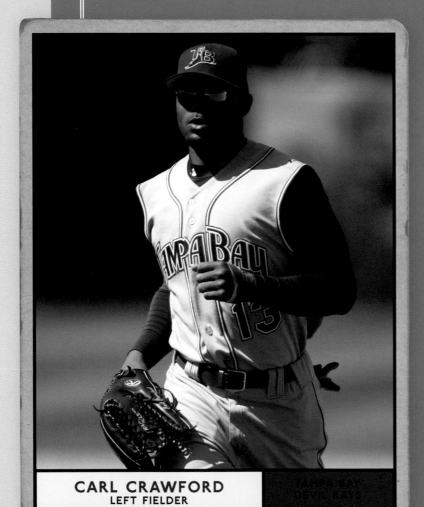

CARL CRAWFORD
LEFT FIELDER

STATS

Devil Rays seasons: 2002–present

Height: 6-2

Weight: 220

- **2004 All-Star**

- **297 career RBI**

- **65 career triples**

- **227 career stolen bases**

barely filling 15,000 seats per home game. As if to rub salt in the wound, Tampa Bay players and fans then watched as the Arizona Diamondbacks— a team born the same year as the Devil Rays—moved onward and upward to win the World Series that season.

In 2002, the Devil Rays started with a bang, winning three straight games against the Detroit Tigers. But dark clouds returned as Tampa surrendered three consecutive games to the mighty New York Yankees and soon thereafter suffered its first no-hitter, losing 10–0 at the hands of Red Sox hurler Derek Lowe at Boston's Fenway Park. The team endured its longest losing streak (15 games) yet before Winn hit a three-run, walk-off home run on May 11 against the Baltimore Orioles to give the Rays a 6–4 victory. "This one was big because it gets the monkey off our back," Winn said. "We were getting a lot of attention for something negative."

Although the Devil Rays, who attracted fewer than a million fans to the home stands all season, finished 2002 in last place again in the AL East with an embarrassing record of 55–106, rising stars seemed to offer some hope for the future. In May, pitcher Joe Kennedy fired a 1–0, complete-game shutout against the Seattle Mariners. Then, in June, Rays pitchers hurled a club-record five complete games.

The team's bats showed signs of heating up, too. Winn represented the Rays at the midseason All-Star Game, going 1-for-2 with a double, a walk, a stolen base, and a run scored. Rookie third baseman Jared Sandberg—nephew of Chicago Cubs Hall-of-Famer Ryne Sandberg—launched two home runs in the same inning against the Los Angeles Dodgers on June 11. The next week, playing in his first major-league games, young outfielder Carl Crawford whacked three triples. Third baseman Aubrey Huff may have been the brightest spot of all, ending the year with 23 home runs and a .313 batting average. Tampa Bay seemed ready to swim out of last place.

100 LOSSES . . . BACK TO BACK

In 2001, the Devil Rays lost 100 games and finished in last place in the AL East with a .383 winning percentage. If fans thought the team could not get any worse, they were wrong. Tampa Bay hit rock bottom the next season by losing 106 games for a .342 percentage. Even more distressing, the 2002 Rays stumbled to the gloomy 100 mark with almost unprecedented speed, losing number 100 by their 148th game on September 14. Only the Washington Senators of 1949 and the New York Mets of 1962 had done it more quickly. "To lose 100 games means you're not very good, that you beat yourself up a lot," admitted Tampa Bay manager Hal McRae. "It means you've got a lot of work to do." It had been more than 20 years since any major-league team had entered the dreaded "Back-to-Back 100-Loss Club." The Toronto Blue Jays became members with terrible seasons in 1977 and 1978, and the Kansas City Royals later joined by accumulating 100-plus losses in 2004 and 2005. Only the 1962 Mets, considered by many people to be the worst team of all time, posted 100 losses before September.

BEN GRIEVE

BEN GRIEVE – Grieve's father, Tom, played nine years in the big leagues in the 1970s. And while Ben's career started in fine style with the Oakland Athletics, he never reached the stardom anticipated in Tampa Bay, his statistics declining over three seasons.

RAYS OF HOPE

efore the 2003 season, the Devil Rays found the man they believed would finally lead them to better things: Tampa native Lou Piniella, one of the most successful managers of the previous decade. Under Piniella's 10-year managerial reign, the Seattle Mariners went 840–711 and reached the AL Championship Series (ALCS) in 1995, 2000, and 2001. The fiery Piniella had also led the Mariners to an AL-record 116 wins in 2001 and captured AL Manager of the Year honors. "I look forward to the challenge, and it's going to be fun," Piniella said upon his hiring. "Managing a baseball team for me is a special privilege, and when you can do it in your hometown, it's even nicer."

After putting Piniella at the helm, the Devil Rays signed some veteran players, including outfielder Al Martin, utility infielder Terry Shumpert, and southpaw pitcher Mike Venafro. The Rays also added two talented rookies to the roster: pitcher Seth McClung and outfielder Rocco Baldelli. McClung added some smoke to the pitching staff with his 97-mile-per-hour fastball, while the 20-year-old Baldelli's hustle and strong hitting earned him the center-field position.

A dramatic, come-from-behind win by the revamped Rays in their 2003 season opener against the Boston Red Sox seemed to trigger a number of

Swift and strong-armed outfielder Rocco Baldelli helped Tampa Bay rise in the standings in 2003 and 2004.

ROCCO BALDELLI

dynamic individual performances. Leading the charge was Baldelli, who won AL Rookie of the Month honors in April by going .364 at the plate and was named to the 2003 Major League Rookie All-Star team. Grieve won the Home Run Derby prior to the annual Hall of Fame Game at Cooperstown, New York, in June, and Crawford tore up the base paths, sprinting to the AL stolen base crown with 55 thefts.

Between July 3 and August 19, the Devil Rays enjoyed some of the hottest hitting and finest pitching in franchise history. Huff racked up 7 home runs and 27 RBI during the stretch, while first baseman Travis Lee and lanky shortstop Julio Lugo launched 6 homers apiece and drove in 17 runs. On the mound, Victor Zambrano went 3–1, while Rob Bell went 2–0. The Rays treated fans to back-to-back shutouts—a first in club history—against the Mariners in September. Even though the team ended up winning seven fewer games than Piniella's stated preseason goal of 70 (and with its worst home attendance yet, an average of 13,070 fans a game) the Rays avoided the dreaded century mark in losses, finishing the 2003 season 63–99.

LOU PINIELLA – As a player, Piniella was a clutch hitter known more for his feistiness than his grace. He maintained that reputation after becoming a big-league skipper in 1986. In his first 19 years of managing, he won 1,519 games and was ejected 71 times.

JULIO LUGO

Julio Lugo swung a hot bat after leaving the Houston Astros for the Devil Rays in the middle of the 2003 season.

CENTER FIELDER · RANDY WINN

A versatile athlete, Randy Winn played college basketball at Santa Clara University before the Florida Marlins selected him in the third round of the 1995 amateur draft. Winn debuted with the expansion Devil Rays as the team's center fielder in 1998. Even though he sometimes had trouble tracking fly balls, his fast feet enabled him to recover and often make astounding defensive plays. Although a quiet, private person off the field who preferred to avoid interviews, Winn spoke volumes as he ripped pitches down the third-base line and into gaps for frequent doubles and triples.

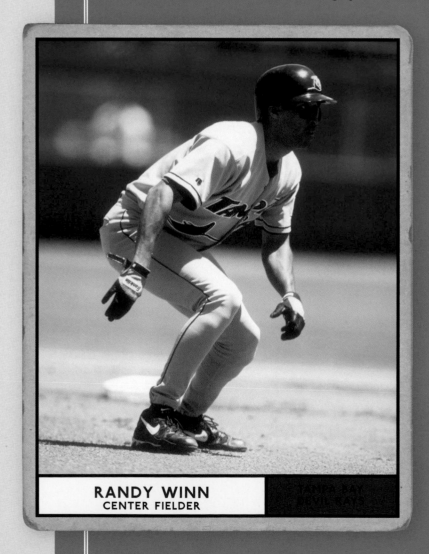

RANDY WINN
CENTER FIELDER

TAMPA BAY
DEVIL RAYS

STATS

Devil Rays seasons: 1998–2002

Height: 6-2

Weight: 195

• **2002 All-Star**

• **80 career HR**

• **457 career RBI**

• **153 career stolen bases**

DEWON BRAZELTON

TAMPA BAY TURNS A TRIPLE

The Devil Rays turned their first triple play in franchise history on September 13, 2002, in the fifth inning against the Toronto Blue Jays at SkyDome. Tampa Bay rookie pitcher Dewon Brazelton, who had climbed to the major leagues from humble beginnings in Tullahoma, Tennessee, stood on the mound in his major-league debut. Blue Jays shortstop Chris Woodward ripped a single, then second baseman Dave Berg was plunked by a wild Brazelton pitch. Next up was center fielder Ken Huckaby, who smacked a line drive at Devil Rays second baseman Andy Sheets. Sheets caught it for the first out,

tossed it to shortstop Chris Gomez (who was covering second base) for the second out, and Gomez turned and fired the ball to first baseman Aubrey Huff, who tagged the bag for the third out before Berg, who had jumped out to a lead, could get back. Prior to that game, the most recent triple play turned behind a pitcher throwing his first major-league game occurred on August 31, 1919, with St. Louis Browns pitcher Rolla Mapel on the mound against the Detroit Tigers. Despite the rare triple putout, the Devil Rays lost the game 5–2.

Hosted by fans in Tokyo, Japan, the Rays won their first game of the 2004 season against the Yankees. Then, in typical Devil Rays fashion, they lost the next day and 28 of the following 38 games. But things then slowly turned around for the Rays. In June, the club won a whopping 20 games, including a franchise-record 12 in a row, thanks largely to the hot bats of switch-hitting right fielder Jose Cruz Jr., Crawford, Lugo, and first baseman Tino Martinez, who had helped the Yankees win four World Series in the late '90s. But then, just as soon as the Rays attained the .500 mark in July—a first for the team— the Yankees put them in their place with a four-game sweep.

The Rays then reverted to their old ways, losing 12 games in a row in September. Still, as bumpy as the road was, Tampa Bay avoided a last-place finish in the AL East for the first time and compiled its best record yet, 70–91. "We've gone from 55 to 70 wins in two years," Piniella said after the season. "What we need to do is not take a step back. We need to keep it going and set a standard for the future."

It seemed for a while that a big step back was inevitable as the Devil Rays' 2005 season opened miserably; halfway through the season, the team lugged a pitiful 28–61 record. But after July, the Rays were buoyed by some outstanding individual play. Lugo produced a .295 hitting average that was tops among

RAYS STING SOX STREAK

It was the season opener at Tropicana Field on March 31, 2003, and the Devil Rays were down 4–1 in the bottom of the ninth inning against the Boston Red Sox. If history had its way, Tampa Bay would lose, as the club had gone 0–10 against the Red Sox at home the year before. But when Devil Rays first baseman Travis Lee hit a leadoff single, and pinch hitter Terry Shumpert followed that up by hitting a belt-high fastball down the left-field line for the game's first homer and two runs, the cursed winds of history began to shift. Rays outfielder Ben Grieve punched another hit for a single, and then pinch hitter Marlon Anderson walked. The Tropicana crowd of 34,391 nervously rose to its feet and cheered as heavy-hitting left fielder Carl Crawford approached the plate. Red Sox closer Chad Fox fired two quick strikes to put Crawford down 0–2 in the count. Staying cool, Crawford fouled off four pitches and then, to the delight of the frenzied fans in attendance, smacked a drive over the right-center-field wall for a 6–4 Devil Rays win. "This was the biggest hit I've ever had," said Crawford.

CARL CRAWFORD

Known for his effortless fastball, lefty
Scott Kazmir was one of the game's
most talented young hurlers.

SCOTT KAZMIR

RIGHT FIELDER · AUBREY HUFF

Good mechanics, enough batspeed to catch up to the fastest fastball, and a knack for spotting breaking balls and changeup pitches made Aubrey Huff one of the steadiest hitters in Devil Rays history. His sweet swing produced 926 hits and 487 RBI for Tampa Bay, and he became the first player in team history to hit 100 home runs. Huff—who bore an uncanny resemblance to late-night television host Conan O'Brien—was a more than capable performer in the field as well, spending time not only in right field, but in left field, at third base, and at first.

AUBREY HUFF
RIGHT FIELDER

TAMPA BAY
DEVIL RAYS

STATS

Devil Rays seasons: 2000–06

Height: 6-4

Weight: 230

- **141 career HR**

- **487 career RBI**

- **.285 career BA**

- **84 extra-base hits in 2003**

MANAGER · LARRY ROTHSCHILD

Larry Rothschild, the first manager in club history, came to the team with winning experience. A 30-year baseball veteran, he wore two World Series rings: one collected as a member of the 1990 Cincinnati Reds coaching staff and the other as a pitching coach for the 1997 Florida Marlins. The Devil Rays' win totals increased in each of their first three seasons under Rothschild's steady hand. A devoted family man known for his patience, Rothschild's skill and friendly rapport with younger players earned him an invitation from New York Yankees manager Joe Torre to join the 2000 AL All-Star team as a coach.

STATS

Devil Rays seasons as manager:
  1998–2001

Height: 6-2

Weight: 180

Managerial Record: 205–294

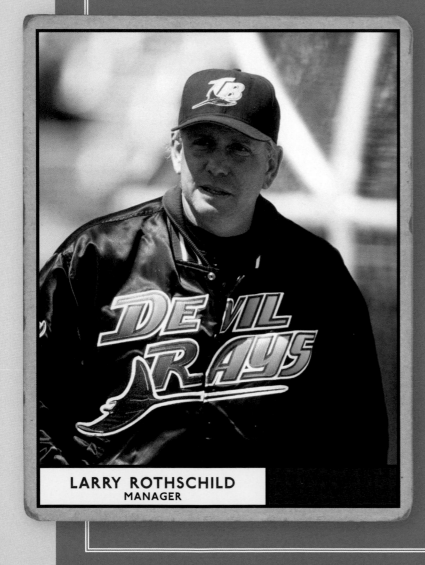

LARRY ROTHSCHILD
MANAGER

all major-league shortstops, Crawford scored a team-leading 101 runs, and third baseman Jorge Cantu homered 28 times and drove in 117 runs. Behind these efforts, the Rays went 39–34 after the All-Star break to finish 67–95.

Tampa Bay regressed to a disappointing 61–101 in 2006, but several young players offered hope that better days were ahead. Crawford ran wild with 58 stolen bases, multitalented outfielder Delmon Young made his big-league debut, and young left-handed pitcher Scott Kazmir emerged as an All-Star by posting 10 wins before being shelved by injury late in the year. The Devil Rays finished the season by losing 16 of their last 20 games. Despite the multitude of losses, Kazmir expressed confidence for team improvement as the 2007 season approached. "We've got a lot of guys coming back who we had last year," he said. "It's going to be fun."

The Tampa Bay Devil Rays' short history is laden with losses, but along the way, rays of hope have broken through the dark clouds. In the earliest seasons, fans could always look to such heroes as Wade Boggs for highlights, and as the Rays approach their 10th anniversary season, sports fans in western Florida today look to a new generation of players with such names as Baldelli, Crawford, and Kazmir in the hopes that Tampa Bay will soon become a harbor of champions.